Spice of Life Cookbook

Spice of Life Cookbook

TROPICAL INSPIRATIONS FOR EVERYDAY NOURISHMENT

Paige Merritt

index

VEGETARIAN AND VEGAN MAIN COURSES

SIDES

DESSERT

Introduction

Being born in Virginia means you grow up eating a lot of home cooked southern meals, having big family barbecues, picking apples and grapes in the fall and blueberries and strawberries in the summer. And then late summer was my favorite time, when we would rig up raw chicken parts in a crab pot and throw them off our neighbor's dock to see if we could catch dinner. Living so close to the Chesapeake Bay area of Virginia certainly had its advantages.

Cartoon-watching did not make up my Saturday mornings like most other children. Instead I would turn on PBS and watch The French Chef with Julia Child, Today's Gourmet with Jacques Pepin, Yan Can Cook, and the Frugal Gourmet. These shows fascinated me and opened up my eyes to international cooking. I would watch with notebook and pen, in hand, to quickly scribble down the recipe and method as it was explained. And with these recipes, I cooked "fancy" dinners on special occasions for family and friends.

When I was young, I had dreams of going to culinary school, but my parents had different education aspirations for me. And although I had been a hostess and waitress in high school, it wasn't until university that I got my first try in a professional kitchen. At first, I started out in the campus dining halls in the dish room which was a labor intensive job for a freshman just trying to have fun at college. But then I slowly got switched around on the schedule to fill the salad bars, make pizzas, grill hamburgers and work the fryer at various dining halls on campus. My first real break as a cook came when ownership changed at the Lebanese restaurant I had been waiting tables at for a couple of years. I had been watching the previous Lebanese owners cook the menu for years and now it was my turn to put what I had learned to the test. I succeeded and enjoyed being in the kitchen very much. And there began my kitchen career.

After a few international trips and attempts to live abroad, I found myself in Northern California working on organic farms. I learned a lot on these farms about growing food and also California style healthy cooking. Yearning for warmer weather, I moved to San Diego where I got my first job as a private chef for a client with a long list of dietary restrictions. I did some intensive self-educating while working with this client and learned about healing with food and diet.

The concrete jungle of San Diego was bringing me down and the real jungle had started to call me back. It had been four years since I first lived in Costa Rica and I knew my time had come to return to that magical country I loved so much. I was only going for a quick vacation before I headed off on a sailboat to circle the world as the onboard chef. As I'm waiting in Panama City to connect with the sailboat, the job was canceled at the very last minute. As I had not planned on being back in San Diego for the next 6-8 months, I went back to Costa Rica and with the help of my friend Hazel, started what became life as I know it today.

APP ETIZ ERS

• • • • • •

Tropical
Ceviche

Seasonal white fish marinated in
citrus juices and coconut milk

Tropical Ceviche

Serves 6

INGREDIENTS

- **300 grams fresh white fish (such as Mahi mahi, sea bass, or red snapper)**
- **¼ cup red onion, diced**
- **½ red bell pepper, diced**
- **½ mango, diced into small cubes**
- **2 cups fresh lime juice**
- **Juice of 1 sweet orange**
- **2 tsp fresh grated ginger**
- **3 tbsp coconut milk**
- **2 tsp Ponzu (Optional)**
- **½ bunch of cilantro chopped ***PRO TIP: Wash and fully dry the cilantro before cutting it. Line all the stalks up and only cut once to reduce bruising)*****
- **Salt to taste (use less if you added ponzu)**

METHOD

1. Dice fish into ¼ inch cubes and mix with lime and orange juices. Allow to marinate in the refrigerator for at least half an hour, but no longer than two hours or the fish will start to get "over cooked."

2. 15 minutes before service time, add the rest of the ingredients and mix well. Adjust seasonings as needed.

3. Serve with tortilla chips, patacones, or crackers.

Shrimp
Ceviche

Parboiled shrimp with watermelon,
jalapeño, and citrus juices

INGREDIENTS

- **300 grams shrimp, cut into ½ inch pieces**
- **¼ cup red onion, diced**
- **½ red bell pepper, diced**
- **3 cups diced watermelon (seeds removed)**
- **¼ diced jalapeno (seeds and veins removed for less heat)**
- **1 tsp grated ginger**
- **½ bunch cilantro, chopped**
- **1 cup lime juice**
- **Juice of 1 sweet orange**
- **½ tsp salt**
- **Chips for serving**

METHOD

1. Store diced vegetables, fruit and citrus juice in the refrigerator until the shrimp are ready to mix in.

2. Fill a saucepan halfway with water and bring to boil.

3. While the water is heating up, fill a large bowl halfway with ice and enough water to cover the ice and set aside.

4. Once the water is boiling, add the shrimp and cook for about one min or until all the shrimp pieces have turned pink.

5. Immediately drain the shrimp and submerge them in the ice bath.

6. Give it a few stirs and then drain the shrimp, discarding any remaining ice.

7. Mix the shrimp, vegetable/fruit mixture, juice and salt.

8. Serve with your favorite chips or crackers.

Shrimp Ceviche

Hearts of Palm
Ceviche

A light and refreshing plant based ceviche
using seasonal vegetables and fruits

Hearts of Palm Ceviche

Serves 8

METHOD

1. Place all ingredients in a bowl and mix well.

2. Adjust salt to taste and allow to marinate in the fridge for half an hour.

3. Serve with tortilla chips.

INGREDIENTS

- 500 grams hearts of palm (canned or already cooked)

- ½ cucumber, deseeded and diced into small cubes

- ⅓ cup red onion, diced

- ½ red bell pepper, diced

- ½ orange or yellow bell pepper

- ½ tomato, deseeded and diced

- 100 grams ground cherries (cape gooseberries), cut in quarters

- ½ jalapeño, deseeded and diced

- 1 bunch of cilantro, chopped

- ½ tsp Salt

- 1 tsp fresh grated ginger

- 1 avocado, diced

- 1 ½ cups lime juice

- Juice of one sweet orange

- Tortilla chips for serving

Tuna Tartare

Raw cubes of tuna marinated in soy,
sesame oil, and ginger sauce

Tuna Tartare

Serves 6

INGREDIENTS

- **400 grams sushi grade ahi tuna**
- **¼ cup poke sauce**
- **4 green onions sliced on the bias, white and light green parts only**
- **⅓ cup mango, diced**
- **⅓ cup avocado, diced**
- **Black and white sesame seeds**
- **Yucca or wonton chips for serving**

Poke sauce:

- **¼ cup soy sauce**
- **1 ½ tsp grated ginger**
- **½ small clove of garlic, smashed into a paste ½ tbsp toasted sesame oil**
- **1 tsp brown sugar**
- **2 tsp rice wine vinegar or lime juice**
- **Pinch of red pepper flakes**

Method

1. Mix all poke sauce ingredients in a jar and shake vigorously until emulsified. Store in the fridge until ready to use.

2. Dice the tuna into ½ inch cubes avoiding as much sinew as possible. *****pro tip:** sinew is the stringy, white, fibrous part that is found in the tuna closer to the tail. It does not fare well to be eaten raw. I try not to include any of that part in my raw poke and prefer to save those parts to lightly sear and throw on top of a salad***

3. Mix green onion, cubed tuna and sauce together.

4. To serve, Stack in a ring mold for individual portions or an 8 inch springform rim for a family style appetizer. Top with mango and avocado, pressing down every layer with a spoon.

5. Unmold and top with sesame seeds. Serve with chips.

Tuna Tataki

Sesame crusted and seared tuna loin
with orange-wasabi mayonnaise

Tuna Tataki

Serves 6

INGREDIENTS

- **400 grams sushi grade ahi tuna**
- **Salt**
- **⅓ cup mixed white and black sesame seeds**
- **3 tbsp vegetable oil**
- **½ cucumber, thinly sliced**
- **Soy sauce for serving**

Orange-wasabi mayo:

- **Juice of ½ orange**
- **⅓ cup mayonnaise**
- **1-2 tsp wasabi paste**
- **½ tsp soy sauce**

METHOD

1. Depending on the size and shape of the tuna, cut down the length of the loin into 3 inch diameter logs and pat dry with a paper towel.

2. Pour sesame seeds on to a rimmed baking sheet large enough to accommodate the length of the tuna pieces.

3. Lightly salt the tuna and roll it in the sesame seeds to evenly coat on all sides.

4. Tightly roll each loin in plastic wrap and place in the Refrigerator for 30 minutes.

5. While the tuna crust is setting, place orange juice, mayonnaise, wasabi paste and soy sauce into a squeeze bottle and shake until completely blended.

6. Heat a nonstick skillet on medium high with 3 tbsp of vegetable oil.

7. As the oil is heating, take the tuna out of the refrigerator and unwrap.

8. Once the oil is shimmering and hot, place the tuna loins in oil and fry on each side for about 1 minute. The goal is to only cook the outside ¼ inch and leave the inside raw.

9. Remove from the frying pan and set it on a wire rack to drain for a few minutes. Pat any excess oil off with a paper towel.

10. Transfer to a cutting board and with a very sharp knife, cut into ¼ inch slices.

11. Arrange the cucumber slice on a plate and top with the sliced tuna. Drizzle wasabi sauce on top and serve the soy sauce on the side.

Chorreadas

Traditional Costa Rican yellow corn pancake
topped with sour cream and mango salsa

INGREDIENTS

- **2 cups sweet yellow corn kernels (traditionally fresh kernels are used but you can substitute canned if fresh is not available)**
- **3 tbsp sugar**
- **Pinch of salt**
- **¼ cup white corn flour (masa)**
- **2 eggs**
- **1 tbsp vegetable oil**
- **½ cup milk**

MANGO SALSA
- **1 large tomato, seeded and diced**
- **1 small mango, diced**
- **¼ cup red onion, diced**
- **½ bunch cilantro washed, dried, and chopped**
- **Juice of 1 lime**
- **Juice of ¼ orange**
- **Pinch of salt**
- **¼ cup sour cream or crème fraiche for serving**

METHOD

1. Mix all mango salsa ingredients together and set aside to marinate.
2. Blend (in a blender or food processor) all chorreada ingredients until mixed well, but not completely smooth (leave a little texture).
3. Heat a non-stick pan over medium-low heat and spray a light coating of oil or use a paper towel to coat the pan evenly.
4. Once the oil is hot, place a large spoonful of the batter into the pan and spread it out into a circle, about 3 inches in diameter and ¼ inch high. repeat to fill the pan.
5. Cook the pancakes for about 4-5 minutes or until golden brown.
6. Use a flexible silicone spatula to work around the edge of the chorreada to release it from the pan and then gently flip it. Cook for another 3 minutes on the other side.
7. Place on a cooling rack. Once all pancakes are cooked you can gently reheat them in a warm oven or microwave.
8. Serve warm or room temperature, topped with a small dollop of sour cream and the mango salsa.

Chorreadas

Platanos
Maduros

Pan fried sweet plantains topped with a lime-cilantro-jalapeno sauce and crumbled queso fresco

Platanos Maduros

Serves 6

METHOD

1. Place all cilantro sauce ingredients into a blender and blend on high for 10 seconds.

2. Heat ¼ inch of vegetable oil in a frying pan over medium heat.

3. While the oil is heating, prepare a sheet pan lined with paper towels or brown paper bags.

4. After the oil begins to shimmer, fill the frying pan with a single layer of the sliced plantains.

5. Once nicely browned, flip and cook them until browned on the other side.

6. Transfer them to the paper-lined sheet pan and repeat the process until all the plantains are cooked.

7. Arrange plantains on a platter in a single layer, spoon sauce over each one and top with crumbled queso fresco.

INGREDIENTS

- 2 ripe sweet plantains sliced ¼ inch thick on the diagonal ***pro tip: look for plantains that are fully yellow and have hints of black spots, but aren't fully soft to the touch like a banana***

- Vegetable oil for frying

- ⅓ cup queso fresco, crumbled

- 1 batch of lime-cilantro-jalapeno sauce

LIME-CILANTRO-JALAPENO SAUCE

- 1/4 jalapeno, without seeds or veins (for a mild version)

- 2-3 limes, juiced

- 1 bunch cilantro, washed and roughly chopped

- 1 small clove of garlic, smashed

- ¼ tsp salt

- 2 tbsp sour cream or ¼ avocado for vegan version

Tortilla Con Queso

White corn masa mixed with fresh farmers cheese and pressed into thick tortillas, topped with refried beans, smashed avocado and pico de gallo

Tortilla Con Queso

Serves 6

INGREDIENTS

- **1 cup white corn flour (masa harina blanco)**
- **1 tsp salt**
- **¾ - 1 cup warm water**
- **¾ cup crumbled queso fresco**
- **½ cup shredded mozzarella cheese**
- **1 can black beans**
- **1 tbsp tomato paste**
- **¼ tsp garlic powder**
- **¼ tsp onion powder**
- **¼ oregano**
- **1 avocado**
- **Juice of 1 lime**
- **1 tomato, diced**
- **¼ red onion, diced**
- **½ bunch cilantro, chopped**

Method

1. In a large bowl, whisk together the masa and the salt.

2. Slowly add the warm water while using your hand as a whisk to mix them together. The consistency should be that of a thick cake batter. Set aside to rest for 10 minutes.

3. Drain the black beans, reserving ¼ cup of the liquid. Add the beans, liquid, tomato paste, garlic, onion, and oregano to a food processor and blend on high until beans are fully mashed. Transfer the mixture to a small saucepan and heat over low heat until bubbling. Turn off heat and cover the saucepan.

4. Mash the avocado with juice from ½ of a lime and a pinch of salt.

5. In a small bowl, mix diced tomato, red onion, cilantro and juice from ½ a lime with a couple pinches of salt.

6. Test the dough by pushing your finger into the middle and feeling the texture. It should be in between firm and soft but not sticky. Adjust with more water or masa accordingly. Once it reaches the firm-soft but not sticky consistency, add the two cheeses and mix them in by hand, slightly kneading the dough.

7. Form the masa into balls slightly larger than a golf ball.

8. Heat a cast iron skillet or comal to medium-high heat and brush with a little vegetable oil.

9. Press a ball of masa in between two pieces of plastic (I use a gallon sized ziplock that has been cut down both sides). Using a plate or anything flat, flatten to about 1/4 inch (these are meant to be thicker than an average corn tortilla used for tacos). Cook on each side until golden brown and some deeper golden spots have formed. Keep them in a tortilla warmer or wrapped in a tea towel until all have been cooked.

10. Serve each tortilla with a layer of beans, avocado and pico de gallo.

Hot Honey Cajun
Shrimp Tostadas

Sweet and spicy buttered shrimp with a
traditional remoulade sauce on a tostada

Hot Honey Cajun Shrimp Tostadas

Serves 8

INGREDIENTS

- 400 grams medium to large sized shrimp, peeled and cleaned
- 4 tbsp salted butter
- 2 tbsp honey
- ¼ tsp cayenne powder
- ½ tbsp Cajun seasoning
- Pinch of Salt (if there is none already in the Cajun seasoning)
- Round Tortilla chips (store bought, or make your own from white corn tortillas fried in vegetable oil) Remoulade sauce

REMOULADE SAUCE
- ¼ cup mayonnaise
- 1 tsp Dijon mustard
- 1 tsp whole grain mustard
- 2 tsp lemon juice
- ¼ lemon zest
- 1 tsp capers
- Dash of Worcestershire sauce
- 1 small clove of garlic

- 1 tbsp finely chopped fresh parsley
- ½ tsp paprika
- Pinch of cayenne
- ¼ tsp salt
- ⅛ tsp black pepper
- Sliced green onion

METHOD

1. Place all remoulade ingredients in a blender and blend on high until fully combined.

2. Melt butter, honey and cayenne powder together in a saucepan on low, stirring to combine.

3. Pat shrimp dry and toss with Cajun seasoning.

4. Increase the heat to medium and add the shrimp. Cook on both sides for about two minutes each or until they are pink all the way through.

5. Lay tortilla chips on a serving platter and put a small dollop of remoulade on each chip. Place one or two shrimp on each chip/tostada and top with green onions. Serve immediately.

Spinach and Hearts of Palm Dip

Baked cream cheese dip with spinach
and chopped hearts of palm

Spinach and Hearts of Palm Dip

Serves 8

INGREDIENTS

- ½ cup cooked spinach
- 1 14oz jar hearts of palm, roughly chopped
- 1 ½ cups cream cheese
- 3 tbsp sour cream
- 3 tbsp grated Parmesan cheese
- ½ tsp garlic powder
- ½ onion powder
- ½ Italian seasoning
- ¼ tsp salt
- ⅛ tsp fresh ground black pepper
- Crostini, crackers, or chips for serving

METHOD

1. Preheat the oven to 375 F.

2. Squeeze out all the excess liquid from the cooked spinach.

3. Add all ingredients to a food processor and process for about 30 seconds.

4. Transfer the mixture into an oven safe baking dish and cover with aluminum foil. Bake for 30 minutes.

5. Remove the foil and bake for another 10 min or broil on low for five minutes to slightly brown the top.

6. Serve warm with crostini, crackers, chips, or pita bread.

Watermelon Salad

Fresh watermelon with goat feta, basil,
toasted pistachios and balsamic reduction

Watermelon Salad

Serves 4

INGREDIENTS

- **4 cups watermelon, cut into cubes or longer "sticks"**

- **15 basil leaves, chiffonade (ribbon cut)**

- **¼ cup goat feta cheese, crumbled**

- **4 tbsp roasted/salted pistachios, chopped**

- **4 tbsp balsamic reduction**

METHOD

1. Bring 1 cup balsamic vinegar to a boil in a small saucepan. Once boiling, reduce heat to low and simmer until it has reduced by half and it coats the back of a spoon.

2. Arrange watermelon cubes on a plate and top with feta, basil, pistachios, and a drizzle of balsamic reduction.

Tropical
Salad

Green salad with mango, corn, black beans, hearts
of palm and avocado citrus dressing

Tropical Salad

Serves 6

Method

1. Place all vinaigrette ingredients, except the olive oil, into a blender and blend until smooth.

2. Add the olive oil and blend for 3 seconds (do not over-blend or the olive oil will become bitter).

3. Toss dressing with lettuce and then top with other ingredients.

INGREDIENTS

- 1 large head of red leaf lettuce washed, dried, and chopped

- ½ mango, peeled and cubed

- 1 can hearts of palm, drained and cut into thin discs

- ½ can black beans, drained and rinsed

- ½ can yellow corn, drained

- Optional add ins: toasted pumpkin seeds, toasted nuts, crispy dried corn kernels, tortilla chips

CITRUS AVOCADO DRESSING

- ½ avocado

- 3 tbsp water

- Juice of 2 limes

- Juice of ½ orange

- ½ tsp Dijon mustard

- 2 tsp honey

- 1 tbsp olive oil

- Salt and fresh ground black pepper to taste

Spinach
Salad

Spinach-based salad with fresh strawberries, candied walnuts, goat feta and balsamic dressing

Spinach Salad

Serves 4

INGREDIENTS

- 1 bunch of spinach, de-leafed
- ½ head of red leaf lettuce
- ½ pint of strawberries (depending on size)
- ¼ cup crumbled goat feta

CANDIED WALNUTS

- 1 cup walnut halves/pieces
- ¼ cup white granulated sugar
- 1 tbsp unsalted butter

BALSAMIC VINAIGRETTE

- ½ cup extra virgin olive oil
- ¼ cup balsamic vinegar
- 1 tsp honey
- 1 tsp Dijon mustard
- 1 clove garlic, minced
- Salt and fresh ground black pepper to taste

METHOD

1. Wash and fully dry the spinach and lettuce leaves. Chop into ribbons and store in the fridge covered with plastic.

2. Wash and dry the strawberries. Slice strawberries lengthwise with or without the tops. ***pro tip: strawberry tops are edible and healthy. They contain vitamin c, calcium, iron and caffeic acid which can help relieve joint pain associated with arthritis***

3. To make the candied walnuts, heat a medium nonstick skillet over medium heat. Add the walnuts, sugar and butter. Stir frequently until sugar starts melting (about 5 minutes). Stir constantly until all sugar has been dissolved and the nuts are coated. Immediately transfer to a parchment-lined baking sheet and separate nuts. Let cool completely.

4. Add all vinaigrette ingredients to a jar and shake vigorously until dressing is emulsified. Save any leftovers for up to a week in the fridge.

5. Toss lettuce, spinach, and ½ of the dressing together in a large bowl. portion on to plates and top with strawberries, feta, and candied walnuts.

FISH AND SEAFOOD MAIN COURSES

. . . . .

Blackened Tuna with Charred Pineapple Relish

Seared tuna steak with a blackened crust topped with a pineapple and ginger relish

Blackened Tuna with Charred Pineapple Relish

Serves 6

INGREDIENTS

- 1 ½ kg fresh Ahi Tuna, cut into 6 steaks and patted dry with a paper towel
- 1 tbsp Blackening seasoning
- 1 batch of pineapple relish
- Vegetable oil

BLACKENING SEASONING

- 1 tsp Salt
- ½ tsp black pepper
- 1 tbsp brown sugar
- 1 tbsp garlic powder
- 1 tbsp onion powder
- 2 tbsp paprika
- 1 tsp cayenne
- ½ tsp dried thyme
- ½ tsp oregano

PINEAPPLE RELISH

- ⅓ of a pineapple peeled and sliced
- ½ tbsp vegetable oil
- ½ small red onion, diced
- ½ small red bell pepper, diced ½ bunch of cilantro, minced 1 tbsp fresh ginger, grated
- 1 clove garlic, minced
- 1 lime, juiced
- 2 tbsp rice wine vinegar
- 2 tsp soy sauce
- ½ tbsp brown sugar

METHOD

1. Preheat a grill on high. Oil the slices of pineapple with vegetable oil and place them on the heated grill.

2. Cook the pineapple on both sides until charred grill marks appear. If you do not have a grill, cook the pineapple slices in a sauté pan on high heat until charred on both sides. Let cool and then dice.

3. Mix ginger, garlic, lime, vinegar, soy sauce and sugar in a jar and shake to mix thoroughly.

4. Pour the dressing over the diced pineapple and the other vegetables and stir. Let the relish marinate at room temperature for about an hour.

5. Preheat a gas grill on medium-high and oil the grates.

6. Mix all blackened seasoning ingredients together and sprinkle about ½ tsp on both sides of each tuna steak.

7. Spray a little vegetable oil on the tuna steaks and Place them on the heated grill.

8. Grill 1-3 minutes on each side, depending on the thickness of the steak and how well you want it cooked.

9. Top the cooked tuna steaks with pineapple relish and serve with cilantro lime rice.

Miso Ahi
Tuna

Seared tuna steaks with a garlic,
ginger, and miso reduction

Miso Ahi Tuna

Serves 4

INGREDIENTS

- 1 kg fresh ahi tuna, cut into 4 steaks and patted dry with a paper towel Salt

- Vegetable oil for cooking

- 3 tbsp sliced green onions 1 tsp white sesame seeds 1 tsp black sesame seeds

MISO SAUCE

- ½ tbsp white miso paste

- 2 tbsp boiling water

- ¼ cup light soy sauce

- 1 tbsp rice wine vinegar

- ½ tbsp brown sugar

- 2 tsp fresh grated ginger

- 1 clove garlic, minced

- ½ tbsp toasted sesame oil

- ½ tsp red pepper flakes

METHOD

1. Whisk the miso paste and boiling water in a small bowl until all miso is dissolved.

2. Put all sauce ingredients in a blender and blend on high for 10 seconds.

3. Transfer the sauce to a small saucepan over medium heat. Bring to a slow boil and continue to cook for 5 minutes. Remove from the heat and set aside.

4. Heat vegetable oil in a skillet over medium high heat.

5. Lightly salt the dried tuna steaks on each side.

6. When the oil is shimmering, add the tuna steaks.

7. Cook for 1-2 minutes depending on the thickness of the steak and how well you want it done.

8. Pour half of the sauce over the top of the steaks and flip, cooking on the second side for another 1-2 minutes.

9. When the tuna is cooked to your liking, plate the tuna steaks on a serving platter and pour the remaining miso sauce on top. Garnish with the sliced green onions and sesame seeds. Serve with sesame-garlic green beans and wasabi mashed potatoes.

Coconut and Almond Crusted Mahi

Mahi mahi filets crusted in shredded coconut and ground almonds, pan fried and served with mango-ginger coulis

Coconut and Almond Crusted Mahi

Serves 6

INGREDIENTS

- **1 ½ kg Mahi Mahi, cut into 6 filets and patted dry**
- **Salt**
- **½ cup flour**
- **2 eggs (add 2 tbsp water), beaten**
- **1 cup shredded coconut (unsweetened)**
- **¾ cup whole raw almonds, pulverized in food processor**
- **Vegetable oil for pan frying**

MANGO-GINGER COULIS

- **1 small mango, peel and seed removed**
- **½ tbsp raw grated ginger**
- **2 tbsp coconut milk**
- **Juice of 1 orange**

Method

1. Set up 3 pie pans or baking dishes: flour in one, the egg wash in the second, and the almond flour mixed with the shredded coconut in the third. Place a fork in each dish to help with the coating process.

2. Sprinkle both sides of the fish with salt.

3. One by one, coat each filet with flour, then the egg wash, and finally with the almond and coconut mixture. Repeat this process for all the fish filets, and then store in an airtight container in the fridge for an hour.

4. Blend all coulis ingredients in a food processor or blender until smooth.

5. Preheat the oven to 350 F.

6. Heat ½ inch of vegetable oil in a nonstick sauté pan over medium-high heat.

7. Working in batches (not to overfill the skillet) carefully place fish filets in the hot oil and fry on each side until a medium golden color is achieved. Place on a baking sheet fitted with a cooling rack.

8. Repeat with all filets and then place in the oven for 5-6 minutes until the internal temperature is 125 F. Omit this step if your fish filets are thin.

9. Serve immediately with coulis on top or on the side. Serve with orange glazed green beans and mashed potatoes.

Mahi with Italian Style Salsa Verde

Pan seared fish topped with basil, mint,
and parsley sauce and diced avocado

Mahi with Italian Style Salsa Verde

Serves 6

INGREDIENTS

- 1 ½ kg Mahi Mahi cut into 6 filets and patted dry
- 1 tbsp olive oil, for frying
- Salt and pepper
- 1 avocado peeled, deseeded, and diced

SALSA VERDE

- ½ cup roughly chopped parsley
- ½ cup roughly chopped basil
- ⅓ cup roughly chopped mint
- ½ tbsp Dijon mustard
- 1 lemon, zested and juiced
- 1 large clove of garlic, smashed
- ½ tbsp anchovy paste
- 1 tbsp chopped capers
- ½ tsp red pepper flakes
- 1 tbsp white wine vinegar
- Salt and black pepper
- ⅓ cup extra virgin olive oil

METHOD

1. Place all sauce ingredients, except olive oil, into a blender and mix until almost smooth.

2. Add the olive oil and continue to blend for 5 seconds. Do not over blend or the olive oil will become bitter.

3. Pour sauce into a bowl and gently mix with the diced avocado. Cover with plastic wrap and set aside to marinate.

4. Heat 1 tbsp of olive oil in a large nonstick skillet over medium-high heat until it shimmers.

5. Sprinkle the fish with salt and pepper on both sides and place them carefully in the hot oil.

6. Cook on the first side, untouched, for about 4 minutes or until a golden brown crust has formed.

7. Flip them over and turn the heat down to medium-low.

8. Cook for another 2 or 3 minutes, depending on the thickness of the filets, until an internal temperature of 125 F is reached.

9. Top the cooked fish with the salsa verde and serve alongside the white bean and cucumber salad and oven roasted baby potatoes.

Banana Leaf
Grilled Fish

Costa Rican style grilled fish wrapped in banana
leaves with chipotle-honey butter and oranges

Banana Leaf Grilled Fish

Serves 4

INGREDIENTS

- **1 kg of fresh white fish (I love red snapper for this recipe)**
- **1 packet of banana leaves **usually can be found in a Latin American market**
- **6 tbsp butter, softened**
- **1 tbsp honey**
- **½ tbsp chipotle paste (or more if you like spicy)**
- **Salt and freshly ground black pepper**
- **4 sweet oranges**
- **Chopped cilantro for serving**

METHOD

1. Heat a grill to 425 F and oil the grates.

2. Whisk softened butter, honey, chipotle paste and 2 tbsp fresh squeezed orange juice until combined.

3. Cut fish into four even filets, pat dry and sprinkle with salt and pepper on both sides.

4. Slice 3 oranges into thin rounds.

5. Lay about a 1 foot long length of banana leaf on the counter and arrange two or three slices of orange about 4 inches from the end of the leaf.

6. Place one fish filet on top of the orange slices. Spread about ½ tbsp of the chipotle butter on top, then cover with two or three more slices of orange.

7. Fold both lengthwise sides of the leaf over the fish. Then fold the short open end over the filet. Roll the filet down the length of the banana leaf to make a square packet with seam side facing down.

8. Repeat this process with all fish filets.

9. Place on the grill and cook for 6 minutes on each side. Check with a thermometer. Cook until internal temp reaches 125 F.

10. Remove from the grill and carefully remove from the banana leaf. Garnish with fresh orange slices, cilantro, and any leftover chipotle butter.

Fish with White Wine,
Cherry Tomato and Basil Broth

Pan seared fish topped with a white wine reduction, blistered cherry tomato, garlic and fresh basil

Fish with White Wine, Cherry Tomato and Basil Broth

INGREDIENTS

- 1 ½ kg white fish filets such as sea bass or cod
- 3 tbsp olive oil
- 1 tbsp butter
- ¼ tsp red pepper flakes
- 4 garlic cloves, minced
- 1 pint cherry tomatoes, washed and cut in half
- ½ bunch basil leaves washed, dried and cut chiffonade
- Salt and black pepper
- 1 tsp sugar
- 1 tbsp lemon juice
- 1/2 tsp lemon zest
- 1/3 cup white wine such as a Sauvignon Blanc

Serves 6

METHOD

1. Preheat the oven to 425 F.

2. Heat 2 tbsp olive oil and 1 tbsp butter in a heavy bottomed saucepan over medium heat.

3. Add red pepper flakes and allow to sizzle for a few seconds.

4. Add the garlic and continuously stir until the aroma of garlic has softened, about 1-2 minutes.

5. Add the cherry tomatoes and simmer until tomatoes are blistered but not falling apart, about 7 minutes.

6. Pour in white wine, sugar, lemon juice and zest, and simmer for another 5-6 minutes.

7. Turn off the heat and stir in half of the basil leaves.

8. Heat an oven safe skillet over medium heat with 1 tbsp of olive oil.

9. Pat the fish filets dry with a paper towel and then sprinkle with salt and pepper. Once the oil is shimmering, add them to the hot pan and cook undisturbed until a golden crust has formed, about 3-4 min.

10. Flip them over and place the pan in the oven to cook for an additional 2-3 minutes, depending on the thickness of the filets.

11. Remove from the oven once the internal temp has reached 125 F.

12. Remove filets from the pan and place on a serving tray. Top with the cherry tomato broth and the rest of the fresh basil. Serve immediately.

Spiced Tomato and Tamarind Fish

Fish simmered with hand-blended curry powder, tamarind and tomato purée

Spiced Tomato and Tamarind Fish

Serves 6

INGREDIENTS

- 1 ½ kg firm white fish filet (such as mahi), cut into 6 filets
- 500 g of tomato purée
- 1 small yellow onion, diced
- 2 tsp grated ginger
- 3 cloves of garlic, crushed
- 1 jalapeño, chopped (white veins and seeds removed for a mild version)
- 1 ¼ cup fresh pressed tamarind juice or 1 tbsp concentrate dissolved in 1¼ cup warm water 1 tsp turmeric powder
- ½ tsp cayenne powder (less for a mild version)
- 2 tsp coriander seeds
- ½ tsp mustard seeds
- ½ tsp cumin seeds
- ½ tsp fennel seeds
- 1 tsp salt, or more to taste
- 1 cup full fat, unsweetened coconut milk
- 10 curry leaves (omit if unavailable)
- 2 tbsp coconut oil
- Cilantro, chopped, for serving

Method

1. Heat a saute pan over low heat and add coriander, mustard, cumin and fennel seeds. Dry toast the spices, swirling the pan until aromatic (about 3 minutes). Remove them from the heat and let cool on a plate. Grind them in a spice grinder or with a mortar and pestle.

2. Heat coconut oil on medium heat in a large heavy-bottomed sauté pan. Add diced onions, and sauté until translucent (about 5 minutes).

3. Add garlic, ginger, and jalapeño and sauté for another 5 minutes.

4. Add spices, tomato purée, coconut milk, tamarind and curry leaves (if using). Simmer for 10 minutes.

5. Remove from the heat. Add to a blender or use an immersion blender to purée. (Be very careful if using a traditional blender with hot ingredients. I usually put a kitchen towel over the lid when blending hot liquids.)

6. Once puréed, return it to the sauté pan and add the fish filets.

7. Cover and simmer over medium-low heat for 5 minutes. Flip the fish and simmer for 5 more minutes.

8. Garnish with chopped cilantro and serve with basmati rice.

Mar y Mar

Seasonal white fish and shrimp with coconut-curried butternut squash sauce

Mar y Mar

Serves 6

INGREDIENTS

- 1 kg white fish filet
- 1 kg medium sized peeled shrimp
- 1 small butternut squash (around 1½ to 2 kg) peeled, deseeded, and cubed
- 1 small yellow onion, diced
- ½ tbsp grated ginger
- 1 ½ tsp garlic paste
- 1 tsp madras curry powder (or your favorite curry blend)
- ½ tsp garam masala
- 3 tbsp fresh orange juice
- 1 tsp salt (adjust accordingly depending on if the vegetable broth is salted, unsalted, or low sodium) 2 cups vegetable broth
- 1 cup coconut milk
- 2 tbsp coconut oil
- 1 tbsp olive oil, divided

METHOD

1. Heat the coconut oil in a heavy-bottomed pot over medium-low heat. Once the oil is shimmering, add the diced onions and cook until translucent.

2. Add the garlic, ginger, and spice powders and cook for 2 minutes more, stirring constantly.

3. Add the butternut squash, broth and coconut milk and cover with a lid. Simmer on low until the squash is fully soft (about 15 minutes).

4. Transfer to a food processor or blender, add the orange juice and salt, and carefully blend (always use caution when blending hot ingredients) until smooth.

5. Heat each ½ tbsp of olive oil in two sauté pans over medium heat.

6. Pat the fish filets and the shrimp dry. Sprinkle with salt.

7. Once the oil is shimmering, add the shrimp to one pan and the fish to the other.

8. Cook the shrimp for roughly 2 minutes on each side until they are pink (the cooking time will depend on the size of the shrimp). Remove from the pan.

9. Cook the fish on the first side until a nice brown crust has formed. Then flip over, lower heat, and cook until a thermometer reads 125 F degrees. Remove from the pan.

10. Re-heat the sauce, if necessary, and then plate the fish with the shrimp on top and finish off with the sauce.

11. Serve with baby potatoes and grilled green onions.

Coconut and Lemongrass Shrimp

Southeast Asian inspired shrimp in a fragrant coconut milk broth

Coconut and Lemongrass Shrimp

Serves 4

INGREDIENTS

- **1200 grams large peeled shrimp**
- **1 cup full fat coconut milk**
- **3 tbsp chopped lemongrass**
- **1 tbsp grated ginger**
- **3 garlic cloves, crushed**
- **½ tbsp fish sauce**
- **¼ cup lime juice**
- **1 tbsp unrefined cane sugar, or brown sugar**
- **½ cup seafood broth**
- **Sliced green onion for garnish**

METHOD

1. Place all ingredients except shrimp and green onion in a blender and blend on high for 20 seconds.

2. Pour sauce into a stock pot and simmer on medium heat for 20 minutes.

3. Strain and place sauce back into the pan, cooking over low heat.

4. Add the shrimp and cook until they have turned pink (about 6 minutes).

5. Serve with rice noodles or jasmine rice and top with green onions. ***pro tip-** turn this into a soup by doubling the sauce ingredients and adding vegetables such as bell peppers, green beans, mushrooms, pumpkin, squash***

Diablo
Shrimp

Shrimp simmered in a spicy tomato
and paprika sauce

Diablo Shrimp

Serves 6

INGREDIENTS

- **1800 grams peeled shrimp**
- **1 14oz jar of tomato purée**
- **2 tbsp extra virgin olive oil**
- **1 small yellow onion, chopped**
- **4 cloves garlic, roughly chopped**
- **1 tsp red chili pepper flakes (less if you want it less spicy)**
- **½ tbsp smoked paprika**
- **2 tsp sugar**
- **1 tsp salt**
- **½ tsp freshly cracked black pepper**
- **Finely chopped parsley for garnishing**

METHOD

1. Heat 2 tbsp olive oil in a heavy-bottomed pot over medium-low heat.

2. Sauté onions in olive oil until they are completely softened and translucent (about 5 minutes).

3. Add the garlic and cook until the fragrance mellows (about 2 minutes).

4. Add chili flakes and smoked paprika and continue to cook for a few more minutes.

5. Transfer this mixture to a blender with the tomatoes, sugar, salt, and pepper and blend until smooth.

6. Return the sauce to the pot and simmer over low heat for about 10 minutes.

7. Add the shrimp and continue cooking until all the shrimp have turned pink (about 5-6 minutes).

8. Garnish with chopped parsley and serve with garlic parmesan pasta or couscous or crusty bread (anything that will soak up the juices).

CHICKEN DISHES

. . . . .

Pineapple
Chicken

Pineapple, paprika and sugarcane-glazed grilled chicken

Pineapple Chicken

Serves 6

INGREDIENTS

- 1 ½ kg chicken breasts, cut into large tenders
- 1 large pineapple, ½ cut into small chunks and ½ cut into slices for the grill
- Juice of 1 large orange
- 3 tbsp natural unrefined cane sugar or brown sugar
- ½ tbsp paprika
- 1 tsp fresh grated ginger
- 1 tbsp ketchup
- ½ tbsp soy sauce
- 1 tsp salt
- ½ tsp cumin
- Vegetable oil
- Chopped cilantro for serving

METHOD

1. Heat a grill to medium high heat and oil the grates.

2. Blend ½ of the chunked pineapple with orange juice, sugar, paprika, ginger, tomato paste, and soy sauce until smooth.

3. Transfer blended sauce to a sauce pan and simmer over low heat for 20 minutes until reduced slightly.

4. Brush the pineapple slices with a little vegetable oil and grill on each side for about 5 minutes until grill marks are formed. Remove and set aside until service time.

5. Mix chicken with salt, cumin powder, a few tablespoons of the sauce, and some vegetable oil.

6. Grill chicken for about five minutes on each side or until a thermometer reads 165 degrees.

7. Remove from the grill and top with the pineapple sauce and cilantro. Serve with pineapple slices, black bean and corn salad, and hearts of palm rice.

Lemon and Thyme Grilled Chicken

Garlic, lemon juice, fresh thyme leaves and olive oil marinated chicken

Lemon and Thyme Grilled Chicken

INGREDIENTS

- 1½ kg chicken breast, cut into six cutlets
- Juice of 3 lemons
- Zest of 1 lemon
- ¼ cup extra virgin olive oil
- 10 garlic cloves, crushed
- 2 tsp salt
- Ground black pepper, to taste
- 3 tbsp fresh thyme leaves

METHOD

1. Place all ingredients in a ziplock bag and marinate for at least 2 hours in the refrigerator.

2. Heat a grill on high and oil the grates.

3. Place chicken on grill and cook evenly on both sides until a thermometer reads 160 F (about 5 minutes on each side).

4. Garnish with extra lemon wedges and thyme leaves. Serve with mashed potatoes and balsamic roasted vegetables.

Peruvian Aji
Verde Chicken

Roasted chicken with a traditional Peruvian
cilantro, jalapeno, and Parmesan sauce

.59.

Peruvian Aji Verde Chicken

Serves 6

METHOD

1. Mix chicken and marinade ingredients in a ziplock and place in the refrigerator for 1 hour.

2. Place all sauce ingredients in a blender and blend until smooth.

3. Heat oven to 400 F and line a rimmed baking tray with parchment paper.

4. Remove chicken from the marinade and pat dry with paper towels.

5. Brush dried chicken legs with olive oil, place on a baking tray skin side up, and bake for 35 to 45 minutes, until the internal temperature reaches 165 F.

6. Allow to rest for 10 minutes, then top with aji verde sauce and serve with yellow rice and vegetable slaw or salad.

INGREDIENTS

- **6 hindquarters (leg and thigh together, depending on the size)**
- **2 tbsp olive oil**

MARINADE
- **10 cloves garlic, minced**
- **¼ cup olive oil**
- **¼ cup lime juice**
- **2 tbsp honey**
- **1 ½ tbsp ground cumin**
- **1 tbsp paprika**
- **1 tsp dried oregano**
- **2 tsp salt**
- **1 tsp ground black pepper**

AJI VERDE SAUCE
- **1/2 cup mayonnaise**
- **1/4 cup sour cream**
- **1 tbsp aji amarillo paste**
- **2 ½ cups chopped cilantro**
- **2 jalapeños, chopped (seeds and veins removed for a mild version)**
- **2 green onions, chopped**
- **2 cloves garlic, smashed**
- **⅓ cup grated Parmesan cheese**
- **1 tbsp vegetable oil**
- **3 tbsp lime juice**
- **¼ tsp sea salt**

VEGETARIAN AND VEGAN MAIN COURSES

Caribbean
Curry

Traditional style Costa Rican coconut and
vegetable curry from the Caribbean side

Caribbean Curry

Serves 6

Method

1. Heat the coconut oil in a stock pot over low heat, and add the whole cumin and coriander seeds.

2. Cook for 2 minutes until the seeds are sizzling and very fragrant. Add the onion and turn heat up to medium, sautéing for another 5 minutes.

3. Add ginger and garlic and stir constantly for 1-2 minutes.

4. Add coconut milk, vegetable broth, curry powder, sugar, salt and habanero pepper (if using) and simmer.

5. While curry is simmering, heat ½ tbsp coconut oil in a saute pan over medium heat. Add the vegetables and saute until browned.

6. Add browned vegetables to the curry. Add lime juice and half of the cilantro and adjust seasonings as needed. Serve with Caribbean style rice and beans and another sprinkle of cilantro on top.

INGREDIENTS

CURRY BROTH
- 1 tbsp coconut oil
- 1 tsp cumin seeds, toasted
- 1 tsp coriander seeds, toasted
- ¼ cup yellow onion, minced finely
- 1 tbsp ginger root, grated
- 4 cloves garlic, minced
- 2 14oz cans coconut milk
- 1 cup vegetable broth
- ½ tbsp spice blend (or store bought madras curry powder with a little added allspice powder)
- 1 tbsp brown sugar
- 1 whole habanero pepper (for a spicy version)
- ½-1 tsp salt, depending on if the broth is salted or not
- Juice of 1 lime
- ½ bunch cilantro, chopped

VEGETABLES
- 6 large portobello mushrooms, sliced
- 1 pint button or baby bellas, washed, dried and sliced
- 1 red onion, thinly sliced
- 2 bell peppers (whichever color you prefer), sliced
- 1 medium carrot, sliced on the bias
- 1 zucchini, cut into quarters lengthwise then cut into 1 inch chunks
- Broccoli, green beans, cauliflower, etc.
- ½ tbsp coconut oil
- 1 tsp curry powder
- ½ tsp salt

CARIBBEAN CURRY SPICE MIX
- 2 tsp coriander seeds
- 2 tsp cumin seeds
- ½ tsp allspice seeds
- ⅛ tsp cardamom seeds
- 1 tsp fenugreek seeds
- 1 tsp yellow mustard seeds
- 1 tsp black peppercorns
- 1 tsp clove
- ½ cinnamon stick (I use Ceylon cinnamon)
- 2 tsp turmeric powder

Curry Spice Method

1. Gently toast all whole spices in a frying pan over low heat, constantly swirling the pan until the spices become frangent.

2. Remove them immediately and transfer to a plate to cool.

3. Once cooled completely, add all spices to a grinder or mortar and pestle and grind into a fine powder.

Stuffed Portobello Mushroom

Balsamic roasted portobello stuffed with goat cheese
and crispy breadcrumbs accompanied by walnut
pesto and roasted red bell peppers

.65.

Stuffed Portobello Mushroom

Serves 4

INGREDIENTS

- 6 to 10 portobello mushrooms, depending on the size
- 1 tbsp balsamic vinegar
- 1 tbsp extra virgin olive oil
- Salt
- black pepper
- ½ tsp garlic powder
- 8 ounces goat chevre
- 1 tsp dried mixed herbs such as parsley, basil, oregano, rosemary, or 2 tsp fresh herbs, minced 4 red bell peppers

WALNUT PESTO

- 1 bunch fresh basil
- ¼ cup raw walnuts
- 1 clove garlic
- ¼ cup Parmesan cheese
- Sea salt
- Fresh cracked pepper
- ¼ cup olive oil

CRISPY BREADCRUMBS

- 1 cup breadcrumbs
- ½ tbsp olive oil
- 2 tbsp butter
- 1 tsp dried Italian herbs ¼ garlic powder

METHOD

1. Preheat the oven to 400 F.
2. Place red bell peppers on a parchment-lined baking sheet and cook on the lower rack of the oven until fully soft, and skins are slightly burnt (about 30 minutes). Remove from the oven, cover with foil, and set aside to cool.
3. To make the breadcrumbs, melt olive oil and butter in a sauté pan over medium heat. Add the breadcrumbs, herbs and garlic powder, and cook, stirring constantly until golden brown. Transfer to a bowl and set aside.
4. Carefully wash and dry the portobello mushrooms. Remove stems (save these for a different use, such as an omelette or stir fry) and gills.
5. Sprinkle the inside with salt and lay them "stem side" down on a baking tray with a wire rack. Brush the tops with olive oil and bake for 15 minutes.
6. Mix goat chèvre with herbs and set aside.
7. Remove mushrooms from the oven and flip. Add the balsamic vinegar and a little olive oil to the inside, and place back in the oven for 5 minutes. Remove and discard any liquid from inside the mushrooms. Stuff with herbed goat chevre, and place back in the oven for 10 minutes.
8. Place all pesto ingredients except olive oil in a food processor and blend (scraping down sides as needed) until fully chopped. Add olive oil and blend until smooth (be careful not to blend for too long or the olive oil will become bitter and ruin the taste of the pesto).
9. Peel and remove the seeds from the roasted bell peppers. Cut into fourths.
10. Remove mushrooms from the oven and top with crispy breadcrumbs. Spread a portion of pesto on each plate, place mushrooms on top, and scatter roasted bell peppers around.

Sesame Crusted Feta
with Honey and Thyme

Baked feta, crusted with sesame seeds, drizzled
with thyme-infused honey

Sesame Crusted Feta with Honey and Thyme

Serves 4

INGREDIENTS

- 2 8 oz blocks of Feta cheese
- ¼ cup flour
- 2 eggs
- 1 tbsp water
- 1 cup mixed sesame seeds (black and white)
- 1 tbsp olive oil
- ⅓ cup honey
- 1 tbsp fresh thyme leaves
- A few thyme sprigs for serving

METHOD

1. Preheat the oven to 425 F.
2. Pat feta dry.
3. Set up flour in one bowl, eggs whisked with water in a second bowl, and sesame seeds in a third.
4. Coat feta with flour, then dredge through egg wash, then sesame seeds.
5. Place feta on an oiled baking tray and spray or drizzle more olive oil on top.
6. Bake in the oven for 25 minutes.
7. While the feta is baking, place honey and thyme leaves in a small pot and simmer on low heat for 5 minutes to infuse the flavors.
8. Check the feta, and If sesame seeds have not browned on top, place under the broiler on low for 2-3 minutes.
9. Remove from the oven when the seeds are browned, and top with the thyme- infused honey. Serve with crusty bread and green salad.

Tandoori Roasted
Cauliflower Wedge

Indian tandoori-style roasted cauliflower
with a chickpea masala curry

Tandoori Roasted Cauliflower Wedge

INGREDIENTS

CAULIFLOWER

- 2 heads of cauliflower
- 1 tbsp salt
- ½ tsp turmeric powder

MARINADE

- ½ cup yogurt
- 2 tbsp lime juice
- 2 tsp garlic paste
- 2 tsp ginger, grated
- 1 tsp garam masala
- ½ ground cumin
- ¼ tsp cayenne
- 2 tsp paprika
- 1 tsp ground coriander
- ½ tsp ground turmeric
- 1 ½ tsp salt
- 1 ½ tbsp olive oil
- 1 tbsp finely chopped cilantro for garnishing

CHICKPEA MASALA

- 2 400g cans of chickpeas, drained
- ½ tbsp vegetable oil
- 1 cup diced yellow onion
- 1 tsp ginger paste
- 1 tsp garlic paste
- 1 tsp cumin seeds
- ½ tsp ground turmeric
- 2 tsp ground coriander
- 1 tsp paprika
- 1 tsp cayenne powder
- 1 tsp garam masala
- 2 tbsp tomato paste
- 1 400g canned diced tomatoes
- 1 tsp lime juice
- ¾ cup heavy cream or coconut milk Water as needed
- 1 tsp salt

Serves 6

METHOD

1. In a large stock pot, boil water (enough to fully submerge the individual cauliflower wedges) with a tbsp of salt and ½ tsp turmeric powder.

2. Remove leaves and trim the stem of the cauliflower heads. Make sure the stem is flush with the bottom of the cauliflower and place stem side down on a cutting board. Cut the cauliflower in half and then in thirds to make 6 wedges per head.

3. Once the water has come to a rolling boil, place as many wedges in the pot as will fit without overcrowding, and boil for 3 minutes. Remove and let all excess water drain off. Repeat for all the cauliflower wedges.

4. Mix marinade ingredients together in a bowl and then rub into cooled cauliflower wedges, making sure to get the marinade into all the nooks and crannies of the florets. Place in the refrigerator to marinate for at least one hour (these can be made a day ahead and put in the fridge to marinate overnight).

5. While the cauliflower is marinating, make the chickpea masala by heating the vegetable oil in a heavy-bottomed stock pot over medium heat and sauté the onions until translucent.

6. Add the garlic and ginger paste and all the powdered spices and stir constantly until the smell of raw garlic has softened (about 5 minutes).

7. Add the tomato paste, and incorporate completely to the onion and spice mixture.

8. Add the canned tomatoes and chickpeas and cook for 15 minutes until the consistency of a stew has been reached. Add water if the stew is too thick.

9. Turn off heat, and stir in the heavy cream and salt. Taste and adjust cayenne and salt level to your liking.

10. Heat oven to 450 F. Place cauliflower wedges on a baking tray and bake in the oven for 30 minutes, turning halfway through to make sure all sides are evenly roasted. If the desired level of browning has not been achieved, then broil on high for 3 minutes on each side.

11. Reheat chickpea masala if necessary, and place heated masala as the base on a plate. Top with cauliflower wedges and garnish with chopped cilantro. Serve with turmeric basmati rice.

Stuffed
Butternut
Squash

Oven-roasted butternut squash stuffed with quinoa, dried cranberries, spinach and walnuts with a balsamic reduction

Stuffed Butternut Squash

Serves 4

INGREDIENTS

BAKED SQUASH
- **2 medium Butternut squash, cut lengthwise**
- **1 tbsp olive oil**
- **Salt**
- **Freshly ground black pepper**

QUINOA
- **1 ½ cups quinoa**
- **3 cups vegetable broth**
- **⅓ cup dried cranberries, roughly chopped**
- **1 bunch of spinach, cut into ribbons**
- **¼ cup toasted walnut pieces**
- **¼ cup crumbled feta cheese**

DRESSING
- **2 tbsp fresh orange juice**
- **¼ cup balsamic vinegar**
- **¼ cup olive oil**
- **1 tsp dijon mustard**
- **¼ tsp garlic powder**
- **Salt and pepper, to taste**

GARNISH
- **4 tbsp balsamic reduction**
- **Optional topping of arugula**

Method

1. Preheat an oven to 400 F.

2. Rub butternut squash halves with olive oil. Sprinkle with salt and pepper and bake until fork tender (about 35 minutes).

3. Put all dressing ingredients into a jar and shake until completely emulsified.

4. Rinse quinoa if not prewashed. Add to a stock pot with the vegetable broth and bring to a boil. Once boiling, turn heat to low, cover and simmer for 18 minutes, or until done.

5. Throw spinach on top of quinoa when cooked, replace the lid and let stand covered for 10 minutes.

6. Remove the lid and fluff the quinoa and spinach together.

7. Mix dressing, cranberries, walnuts, and feta into the quinoa.

8. Stuff quinoa mixture into butternut squash halves, then top with balsamic reduction and arugula.

SIDES
· · · · ·

Corn and Black Bean Salad

Serves 6

INGREDIENTS

- 1 15oz can corn kernels (or fresh charred kernels)
- 1 15 oz can black beans, drained and rinsed
- 1 small tomato, deseeded and diced
- ¼ bell pepper, diced
- ¼ red onion, diced
- 3 tbsp cilantro, chopped
- ¼ jalapeño diced, seeds and veins removed (depending on spice level you prefer)

DRESSING

- 2 tbsp lime juice
- 2 tbsp apple cider vinegar
- 2 tbsp olive oil
- ¼ tsp chili powder
- ⅛ tsp garlic powder
- Pinch of ground cumin
- 1 tsp sugar
- 1 tsp Dijon mustard
- Pinch (or more) cayenne

METHOD

1. Place all dressing ingredients in a jar with a lid and shake vigorously until emulsified.

2. Place all salad ingredients in a large bowl and mix together with dressing.

3. Cover and chill for at least an hour before serving.

INGREDIENTS

- **1 kg potatoes, peeled**
- **3 tbsp salt**
- **8 tbsp salted butter at room temperature**
- **¼ cup whole milk at room temperature**
- **2 tbsp sour cream at room temperature**
- **Salt**
- **⅛ tsp garlic powder**
- **1 tbsp wasabi paste (or omit for regular mashed potatoes)**

METHOD

1. Fill a large pot with water and 3 tbsp of salt.

2. Wash and peel potatoes.

3. Cut into fourths or any evenly shaped large chunks. Rinse again.

4. Place in a large pot and boil over high heat until the potatoes are soft. Check doneness by stabbing the middle of a potato chunk with a fork. If it easily slides off the fork by itself then they are done.

5. Drain immediately, place back in the pot and cover for 7 minutes.

6. Mash or use a ricer to obtain your desired consistency and mix with remaining ingredients.

Wasabi Mashed Potatoes

Oven Roasted Baby Potatoes

Serves 6

INGREDIENTS

- **1 kg baby potatoes**
- **2 tbsp olive oil**
- **1 tbsp butter**
- **1 tsp Italian seasoning**
- **¼ tsp garlic powder**
- **Salt and pepper**
- **Heavily salted water for boiling**
- **Parsley for serving**

METHOD

1. Wash all dirt off baby potatoes and cut in half (or quarters, depending on size).

2. Place in a pot of heavily salted water (water should fully cover the potatoes). Bring to a boil for about 10 minutes or until the potatoes are easily pierced with a fork.

3. Drain immediately. (This can be done up to a day ahead).

4. Nearer to service time, preheat an oven to 425 F. Toss the baby potatoes with oil, Italian seasoning, salt and pepper.

5. Cook on a parchment lined sheet pan for about 30 minutes or until desired browness is achieved.

6. Transfer the potatoes to a large bowl, and toss with garlic powder and butter. Top with parsley and serve immediately.

Orange Glazed Green Beans

Serves 6

INGREDIENTS

- 1 kg green beans, trimmed
- 1 tbsp olive oil
- Juice of 1 orange
- 1 clove garlic
- 2 tsp dijon mustard
- 2 tsp honey
- 1 tsp balsamic vinegar
- 1 tsp soy sauce

Method

1. Fill a large stock pot with heavily salted water and bring to a boil.

2. Add the trimmed green beans and cook for about 2 minutes.

3. When they have turned bright green, remove from the heat and drain immediately.

4. Put all dressing ingredients into a jar with a lid and shake vigorously until emulsified.

5. In a large saute pan bring the dressing to a simmer over medium heat and cook until reduced by half.

6. Add the beans and turn the heat to high, sautéing until the beans start to blacken and the sauce has fully reduced to coat the beans.

Sesame Garlic Green Beans

Serves 6

INGREDIENTS

- 1 kg green beans trimmed
- 1 tbsp toasted sesame oil
- 4 cloves garlic minced
- 2 tbsp light soy sauce
- ½ tbsp rice wine vinegar
- ½ tbsp brown sugar
- 1 tsp fresh grated ginger
- 1 tbsp mixed sesame seeds

METHOD

1. Fill a large stock pot with heavily salted water and bring to a boil.

2. Add the trimmed green beans and cook for 2 minutes.

3. When they have turned bright green, remove from the heat and drain.

4. Put all dressing ingredients into a jar with a lid and shake vigorously until emulsified.

5. In a large saute pan bring the dressing to a simmer over medium heat and cook until reduced by half.

6. Add the beans and turn the heat to high, sautéing until the beans start to blacken and the sauce has fully reduced to coat the beans. Garnish with more sesame seeds.

Cucumber, Cherry Tomato and White Bean Salad

INGREDIENTS

- **1 quart cherry tomatoes, quartered**
- **1 cucumber**
- **1 15 oz can cannellini beans, drained and rinsed 2 tbsp finely minced red onion**
- **2 tbsp finely chopped parsley**
- **2 tbsp finely chopped basil**
- **½ tsp dried Italian herbs**

DRESSING

- **2 tbsp white wine vinegar**
- **3 tbsp olive oil**
- **½ tsp Dijon mustard**
- **¼ tsp garlic powder**
- **Salt and fresh ground black pepper**

METHOD

1. Place all dressing ingredients in a jar with a lid and shake vigorously until emulsified.

2. Peel cucumber and cut lengthwise. Remove seeds and cut in half again lengthwise.

3. Chop into small pieces and mix with the tomatoes, cannellini beans, red onion, and herbs.

4. Stir in the dressing and let marinate covered in the fridge for at least an hour before serving. If serving alongside the mahi, bring the salad to room temperature before plating.

Pan Fried Sweet Plantains

Serves 6

INGREDIENTS

- **3 ripe sweet plantains**
- **Vegetable oil or refined coconut oil**
- **Salt**

METHOD

1. Heat ¼ inch of oil in a heavy bottomed saucepan over medium heat.

2. Peel the plantain, and slice on the diagonal to make 1 cm wide pieces.

3. Fry in hot oil on both sides until brown, then place on a paper-towel lined cookie rack and sprinkle with salt.

4. Repeat for all the plantains and reheat in an oven if needed before service.

Herbal Quinoa

Serves 6

Method

1. Bring all ingredients (except the fresh herbs) to a boil in a large covered stock pot.

2. Reduce heat to low and simmer for about 20 minutes or until all the water has been absorbed.

3. Remove from heat and let sit for another 5 minutes covered.

4. Fluff with a fork and mix in the fresh herbs.

INGREDIENTS

- **2 cups quinoa, rinsed and drained (if not already prewashed)**
- **4 cups vegetable broth**
- **Salt (depending if the vegetable broth is salted or unsalted)**
- **1 tsp Italian seasoning**
- **¼ tsp garlic powder**
- **¼ tsp onion powder**
- **1 tbsp olive oil or butter**
- **¼ cup mixed fresh parsley and basil, finely chopped**

Coconut and Turmeric Basmati Rice

Serves 6 to 8

INGREDIENTS

- **2 cups basmati rice, rinsed and drained**
- **3 ½ cups of water**
- **1 tsp salt**
- **1 tbsp coconut oil**
- **1 tsp mustard seeds**
- **1 small onion, diced**
- **1 clove garlic, minced**
- **1 tsp fresh grated ginger**
- **2 tsp turmeric powder**
- **2 cups coconut milk**
- **1 tbsp chopped curry leaves (omit if not available)**
- **3 tbsp finely chopped cilantro**

METHOD

1. Cook basmati rice with 3½ cups water and 1 tsp of salt in a rice cooker or on the stove top according to box directions. Fluff with a fork once fully cooked.

2. Heat coconut oil on low in a large saucepan and add the mustard seeds. Cook until mustard seeds start popping.

3. Add the onions and increase heat to medium. Cook until onions are translucent.

4. Add garlic and ginger and cook for 5 more minutes.

5. Add the rice and stir to combine all ingredients very well.

6. Add the turmeric powder and stir until all grains of rice are covered.

7. Add the coconut milk and curry leaves and stir to combine. Continue to stir while cooking until all the coconut milk has been absorbed by the rice.

8. Remove from heat and top with cilantro.

Garlic Buttered Parmesan Pasta

INGREDIENTS

- 600 grams pasta of your choice
- 8 tbsp salted butter
- 5 cloves garlic, minced
- 3/4 cup fresh shredded Parmesan cheese
- 3 tbsp parsley, finely chopped
- Salt and fresh ground black pepper

METHOD

1. Cook pasta according to directions in a pot of salted water. Make sure to reserve a cup of the cooking water when draining the pasta.

2. Melt butter and garlic together in a small sauce pot and cook on low for 5-7 minutes or until the smell of raw garlic has dissipated.

3. Place the drained pasta back in the pot and add the garlic butter, Parmesan cheese and black pepper. Stir until everything is combined, using a little pasta water if necessary.

4. Top with parsley and serve immediately.

Serves 6

Caribbean Style Rice and Beans

Serves 8

INGREDIENTS

- 2 cups white rice
- 1½ cups red beans (cooked) drained but with liquid reserved
- 1 small yellow onion, diced
- 2 bay leaves
- 3 stalks fresh thyme
- ½ tsp allspice
- 1 ½ tsp cumin powder
- 1 tbsp freshly grated ginger
- 4 cloves garlic
- 1 whole scotch bonnet pepper, or sub ¼ tsp cayenne for less heat, or hot sauce of your choice
- 1 can (14 oz) coconut milk
- 2 tbsp finely shredded coconut (unsweetened)
- Approximately 1 cup vegetable or chicken broth
- 1 tbsp vegetable oil
- salt
- Chopped cilantro for serving

METHOD

1. Rinse and drain the rice.

2. Heat vegetable oil in a heavy-bottomed stock pot over medium heat.

3. Add the onion and saute until translucent.

4. Add the garlic, ginger, herbs, and spices and sauté for another 5 minutes.

5. Add rice and mix constantly for another 5 minutes to lightly toast the rice.

6. Add the cooked red beans, scotch bonnet or hot sauce, and coconut flakes.

7. Measure out and add 3 cups of liquids: coconut milk, red bean liquid, and vegetable or chicken broth. Stir well.

8. Let rice come to a boil over high heat, then cover and lower heat to a simmer.

9. Let simmer for about 18 minutes or until the rice is fully cooked. Remove from heat and let stand for 5 more minutes and then fluff with a fork. Top with cilantro and serve.

Hearts of Palm Rice

Serves 6

INGREDIENTS

- **2 cups white rice**
- **3 ½ cups vegetable broth**
- **4 tbsp butter (or 2 tbsp olive oil if vegan)**
- **¼ tsp garlic powder**
- **¼ tsp onion powder**
- **Salt (depending if the broth is salted or not)**
- **28 oz can heart of palm, drained and finely chopped**
- **10 oz mozzarella cheese, grated**
- **Cilantro chopped for serving**

Method

1. Rinse rice in a sieve until the water runs clear.
2. Place rice, broth, butter, spices, and chopped hearts of palm into a stock pot and bring to a boil over high heat.
3. Once boiling, lower the flame to low and cover the pot.
4. Preheat the oven to 350 F.
5. Let the rice cook for about 15 minutes or until it has soaked up all the broth.
6. Remove from heat and let stand 5 minutes.
7. Uncover and fluff the rice with a fork.
8. Place rice in an oiled casserole dish and cover with grated cheese.
9. Bake until all cheese is melted. Top with cilantro and serve.

Balsamic Roasted Vegetables

Serves 8

INGREDIENTS

- 1 small head of broccoli, cut into large florets
- 1 bunch mini carrots, split lengthwise
- 1 pint mushrooms, cleaned and cut in halves, quarters, or not at all depending on size (make sure that they are all roughly the same size)
- 2 red bell peppers, chopped into large chunks
- ¼ head cauliflower, cut into medium sized florets
- 1 red onion, cut in chunks
- ½ tbsp italian or Mediterranean spices
- Salt and black pepper
- 3 tbsp olive oil
- 3 or so tbsp balsamic vinegar

METHOD

1. Preheat the oven to 400 F.

2. Toss each vegetable separately with part of the olive oil, balsamic and spices.

3. Line 2 baking sheets with parchment paper for easy cleanup and spread vegetables on baking sheet in a single layer, keeping them separate from each other. ***Pro tip: keeping them separate from one another makes it easier to remove vegetables that are done before others, for example, broccoli cooks faster than cauliflower.***

4. If cooking on separate racks, make sure to switch the baking pans every 15 minutes. Cook until edges are browned and caramelized (about 30 minutes for carrots and cauliflower and slightly less for the others).

Yellow rice

Serves 6

- **2 cups white rice, rinsed and drained**
- **3 ½ cups vegetable broth**
- **2 tsp olive oil**
- **½ cup chopped onion**
- **2 garlic cloves, minced**
- **Salt (depending on if the vegetable broth is unsalted)**
- **1 tsp achiote (annatto) powder or paste**
- **1/4 tsp turmeric**

METHOD

1. Heat oil in a stock pot over medium heat. Add the onions and sauté until translucent
2. Add the garlic and cook for another minute.
3. Add the rinsed rice and stir constantly to toast for about 3 to 5 minutes.
4. Add the broth and achiote and bring to a boil.
5. Once boiling, turn heat to low, cover the pot and cook for about 15 minutes until the rice is fully cooked.
6. Remove from heat and keep covered for 5 minutes before fluffing the rice with a fork.

Blue Cheese Stuffed Tomatoes

Serves 6

METHOD

1. Preheat an oven to 400 F.

2. Cut the Roma tomatoes in half lengthwise and remove seeds.

3. Mix bread crumbs, Parmesan and herbs together.

4. Crumble blue cheese into the breadcrumb mixture and work together with your fingers.

5. Fill the tomatoes with the bread crumb mixture and place on a baking tray.

6. Bake for 20 min or until the tops have browned slightly. Garnish with chopped parsley

INGREDIENTS

- 6-9 Roma tomatoes, depending on size
- 4 oz (100g) blue cheese
- ½ cup unseasoned bread crumbs
- 2 tbsp grated Parmesan
- 1 tsp Italian herbs
- ⅛ tsp garlic powder
- ⅛ tsp salt
- ⅛ tsp black pepper
- Chopped parsley for serving

Cilantro Rice

Serves 6

INGREDIENTS

- **2 cups white rice, rinsed and drained**
- **3 ½ cups vegetable broth**
- **3 tbsp butter or olive oil**
- **¼ cup lime juice**
- **3 tbsp sour cream**
- **1 clove garlic, minced**
- **1 bunch cilantro, roughly chopped**
- **Optional chopped jalapeño**
- **Salt**

METHOD

1. Add rice, vegetable broth and butter to a pot and bring to a boil over high heat.

2. Cover and lower heat to low. Simmer for 18 minutes or until rice is done.

3. Remove from heat and let stand for 5 minutes before fluffing.

4. Add lime juice, sour cream, garlic, cilantro, salt and jalapeno to a blender and process until smooth.

5. Mix into the rice and serve immediately.

DE
SS
ERT
. . . . .

Coconut
Macaroons

Makes about 20 cookies

INGREDIENTS

- **200 gram shredded unsweetened coconut**
- **¼ cup condensed milk**
- **1 egg white**
- **Pinch of salt**
- **¼ tsp vanilla extract**

METHOD

1. Preheat an oven to 375 F.

2. In a medium-sized bowl mix together condensed milk, shredded coconut, vanilla, and salt until fully combined.

3. In a separate bowl, whip the egg white with an electric beater until stiff peaks form.

4. Fold in the egg white to the coconut mixture.

5. Line a baking tray with parchment paper and, using a spoon, scoop balls (with about a 1.5 inch diameter), forming them as needed with the help of another spoon or your fingers. Place them about ½ inch apart on the parchment paper.

6. Bake for 7 minutes, then flip the position of the tray and bake for another 7 minutes or until the tops and edges are beginning to brown.

7. Slide the parchment paper, with cookies, onto a cooling rack for 20 min or until completely cooled. Store in an airtight container until ready to serve.

Coconut Macaroons

Key Lime
Pie

.95.

Key Lime Pie

Serves 12

INGREDIENTS

- 1½ cups ground graham crackers
- ⅓ cup granulated sugar
- 5 tbsp butter, melted
- 1 cup lime juice
- 2 13.5oz cans of condensed milk
- 5 egg yolks
- Whipped cream, lime slices and toasted coconut for serving

METHOD

1. Preheat the oven to 350 F.

2. Melt 5 tbsp of butter in a saucepan.

3. Place about 6 ounces of graham crackers in a food processor and grind until it reaches a powder consistency.

4. Place 1½ cups graham cracker powder, melted butter and granulated sugar in a bowl and mix to combine.

5. Line the bottom of a 9in springform pan with parchment paper and then attach the rim.

6. Empty graham cracker mixture into the springform pan, and press about 1 inch up the sides and firmly down on the bottom to form a crust.

7. Bake in the oven for 10 minutes. Remove and place on a cooling rack.

8. Whisk together the lime juice, condensed milk, and egg yolks in a large bowl. When completely combined, tap the bowl on the counter a few times to bring all air bubbles to the surface to pop.

9. Pour the lime mixture into the crust and bake for 20 min.

10. Remove from the oven and let completely cool on a wire rack.

11. Place in the refrigerator for at least 4 hours to set. Once set, remove from the springform pan and cut into 12 pieces.

12. Serve with whipped cream, toasted coconut, and a slice of lime.

Coffee Tres
Leches Cake

Coffee Tres Leches Cake

Serves 12 to 16

INGREDIENTS

- **1 cup all purpose flour**
- **1 ½ tsp baking powder**
- **¼ tsp salt**
- **5 large eggs, separated**
- **1 cup granulated sugar**
- **⅓ cup milk**
- **1 tsp vanilla extract**
- **12 oz can evaporated milk**
- **14 oz can sweetened condensed milk**
  ¼ cup whole milk
- **1 tbsp instant coffee**
- **Whipped cream**
- **Cinnamon**

Method

1. Preheat the oven to 350 F. Line a 9x13 pan with parchment paper on the bottom. Grease the side of the pan with non-stick cooking spray or butter.

2. In a medium bowl, combine flour, baking powder, and salt.

3. Separate egg yolks from whites in two different bowls.

4. Add 3/4 cup sugar to the egg yolks and mix on high speed until the yolks are a pale yellow.

5. Add ⅓ cup milk and vanilla to the yolk mixture and stir to combine. Pour the yolk mixture over the flour mixture and gently stir until just combined.

6. Beat the egg whites on high with electric beaters. As the whites begin to form peaks, slowly mix in the remaining ¼ cup of sugar.

7. Gently fold the egg whites into the batter to combine thoroughly.

8. Pour batter into the prepared pan and smooth the top if necessary. Bake for 25-30 minutes or until a toothpick inserted in the center comes out clean.

9. Remove and let cool completely.

10. Mix 1 tbsp of instant coffee with a few drops of hot water to dissolve the crystals. Mix with evaporated milk, condensed milk and whole milk.

11. Once cooled, use a skewer to poke holes all over the top of the cake.

12. Slowly pour the milk and coffee mixture over the top of the cake, letting it soak into all the holes and the sides. Refrigerate for at least one hour.

13. Top with whipped cream and cinnamon.

Caramelized
Banana Bread
Pudding

.99.

Caramelized Banana Bread Pudding

Serves 9

INGREDIENTS

- **4 to 6 bananas, depending on size**
- **2 oz rum**
- **3 tbsp granulated sugar**
- **1 loaf brioche bread, torn or cut into 1 in pieces (about 400 g)**
- **13.6 oz can of full fat coconut milk**
- **3/4 cup whole milk**
- **1 cup sweetened condensed milk**
- **2 tbsp butter, melted**
- **2 eggs**
- **1 tsp vanilla extract**
- **½ tsp salt**
- **½ tsp cinnamon**
- **¼ tsp nutmeg**

METHOD

1. Peel and slice all but two of the bananas into coins. Cut two of the bananas in half lengthwise then crosswise. Place them in a bowl and pour rum and sugar over them. Allow to marinate for at least an hour or overnight.

2. Preheat the oven to 350 F.

3. Mix together coconut milk, whole milk, condensed milk, melted butter, vanilla, salt and spices in a large bowl

4. Add bread pieces and soaked banana coins (reserving the long banana slices). Mix well and let sit for at least 1 hour to allow the bread to soak up all the liquid.

5. Grease an 8x8 square baking dish and add the bread mixture. Arrange the sliced bananas on top.

6. Bake for 45 min-1 hour or until the top is golden brown and caramelized. If the browning happens too fast, cover with aluminum foil until fully cooked. Enjoy with whipped cream or ice cream.

Espresso Brownie
with Coffee Glaze

Espresso Brownie with Coffee Glaze

INGREDIENTS

- **10 tbsp unsalted butter**
- **1 ¼ cups granulated sugar**
- **3/4 cups plus 2 tbsp unsweetened cocoa powder**
- **¼ tsp sea salt**
- **1 tsp vanilla extract**
- **2 large cold eggs**
- **½ cup all purpose flour**
- **½ cup sweetened condensed milk**
- **1 tbsp instant coffee (split in two ½ tbsp portions) and a few drops of hot water**

METHOD

1. Preheat the oven to 325 F. Line an 8x8 inch square baking pan with parchment paper, bottom and sides.

2. Set up a double boiler and simmer water, Making sure the water level does not touch the bottom of the top bowl.

3. Combine butter, sugar, cocoa, ½ tbsp instant coffee and salt in the top bowl and stir until melted.

4. Remove from the double boiler and set aside to cool for 5-10 minutes. You want the mixture warm but not hot.

5. Stir in vanilla.

6. Add eggs one at a time, stirring to fully incorporate after each addition.

7. Sift flour into the mixture and stir about 50 times with a large spoon.

8. Spread batter into prepared pan and bake for 20-25 minutes. Test by sticking a toothpick in the center. It should come out with a few moist crumbs.

9. Remove the pan from the oven and set on a wire rack to cool completely.

10. Mix a few drops of hot water with the instant coffee to dissolve crystals. Stir into the condensed milk and incorporate completely. Pour over the top of the brownies.

Pineapple
Flambé

Pineapple Flambé

Serves 8

INGREDIENTS

- 1 large pineapple, cut into small cubes 4 tbsp butter
- 3 tbsp brown sugar
- ¼ tsp nutmeg
- ¼ tsp cinnamon
- ¼ cup aged rum
- Ice cream for serving

METHOD

1. Melt butter in a large sauté pan on medium-low heat.

2. Add in brown sugar and spices and stir to combine.

3. Add pineapple and stir to coat the pineapple with the butter and sugar mixture. Turn heat to high.

4. Stir occasionally until all the pineapple has been caramelized.

5. Add the rum and carefully light on fire.

6. Swirl the pan until the fire has subsided and cook for an additional 5 minutes.

7. Serve hot with vanilla ice cream, caramel sauce, and/or toasted coconut

Chocolate
Almond Tart

Chocolate Almond Tart

Serves 12

INGREDIENTS

- **200 grams whole almonds**
- **¼ cup coconut oil, melted**
- **1 ½ tbsp maple syrup or honey**
- **10 ounces dark chocolate, finely chopped**
- **1 cup full fat canned coconut milk**
- **Toasted shredded coconut, fruit, whipped cream, ice cream for garnish**

Method

1. Add almonds to a food processor and process until pulverized into small bits, but not into a powder

2. Add the melted coconut oil and maple syrup to the almonds and process until combined.

3. Line the bottom of a 9 inch springform pan with plastic wrap and then attach the rim.

4. Press the almond mixture into the bottom of the pan to form an even crust

5. Heat 1 cup coconut milk in a saucepan until bubbling.

6. Place chopped chocolate in a large bowl and pour hot coconut milk on top.

7. Let it sit undisturbed for 5 minutes, then whisk gently until all the chocolate has melted.

8. Tap the bowl a few times on the counter to pop any air bubbles that might have formed while whisking.

9. Pour the chocolate mixture on top of the almond crust and refrigerate for at least 4 hours.

10. Once completely set, warm the sides of the springform pan with a hot wet towel to easily remove it. Remove the bottom of the pan and set the pie on a cutting board. Heat a knife and cut 12 pieces. Serve with toasted coconut, fresh berries, whipped cream, and/or ice cream.

THANK
YOU

· · · ·

Photography by

Paige Merritt and Sarah Yunker

Book design by

Michael Ferrero

www.ingramcontent.com/pod-product-compliance
Lightning Source LLC
Chambersburg PA
CBHW041455120626
46547CB00003B/448